TO: _____

FROM: _____

DATE: _____

Foreword

Black holes in space are a bit of a mystery: They have a mass so great, and a gravitational pull so strong, that even light cannot escape them. When an object hurtles past a black hole's "event horizon" (an invisible boundary that marks a gravitational point of no return), that object will be irretrievably captured. There is no going back.

In Romans the Apostle Paul tells us that everything in the created world is a metaphor for God's "invisible qualities, his eternal power and divine nature" (Romans 1:20). So, what if the dynamics of a black hole are a metaphor for our relationship with Jesus? What if our intentional movement toward him propels us past his "event horizon," making the gravitational pull of his orbit feel like a tractor beam? And what if this close orbit of Jesus finally restores the intimacy with God we were created to enjoy?

When Jesus drove away all the crowds that had been following him by insisting that they "eat his body and drink his blood," he asked his closest friends if they were going to abandon him as well. Because Peter had already crossed his own event horizon with Jesus, he answered this way: "Lord, to whom would we go? You have words that give eternal life" (John 6:68).

This is the response of a black-hole disciple of Jesus—one who is "ruined by him, and ruined for him." That person's life, forever going forward, will be characterized by intimacy with Jesus. And that life is possible for you as well, if you will allow this journal to propel you past his event horizon.

Rick Lawrence
General Editor, *Jesus-Centered Bible*
Author, *The Jesus-Centered Life*

How to Use This Journal

Drawn closely into Jesus' orbit—that's where life is both
happiest and most exciting.

Expect to meet Jesus in fresh ways as you ponder passages
pointing to him from both the Old and New Testaments.
Ask what these verses can help you discover about Jesus...
yourself...and your growing friendship with Jesus.

Just as in the *Jesus-Centered Bible*, blue passages
are those from the Old Testament that point to Jesus,
and red passages are those from the New Testament.

So journal well. Think deeply...doodle playfully...
let your imagination send you soaring.

It's all good—because the Jesus who holds words of
life and truth is eager to meet you anywhere, anytime.

J. John 1:14—So the Word became human and made his home among us. He was full of unfailing love and faithfulness. And we have seen his glory, the glory of the Father's one and only Son.

Romans 10:9—If you openly declare that Jesus is Lord and believe in your heart that God raised him from the dead, you will be saved.

2 Corinthians 12:7b-9a—I was given a thorn in my flesh…Three different times I begged the Lord to take it away. Each time he said, "My grace is all you need. My power works best in weakness."

_____

_____

_____

_____

_____

_____

_____

_____

_____

_____

_____

_____

_____

_____

_____

_____

_____

_____

_____

_____

_____

_____

(J.) Philippians 2:6-8—Though [Jesus] was God, he did not think of equality with God as something to cling to. Instead, he gave up his divine privileges; he took the humble position of a slave and was born as a human being.

_____
_____
_____
_____
_____
_____
_____
_____
_____
_____
_____
_____
_____
_____
_____
_____
_____
_____
_____
_____
_____
_____
_____

J. John 8:57-58—The people said, "You aren't even fifty years old. How can you say you have seen Abraham?" Jesus answered, "I tell you the truth, before Abraham was even born, I am!"

Jesus-Centered Journal

New Living Translation

Copyright © 2015 Group Publishing, Inc.

Visit our websites: group.com and jesuscenteredlife.com

Scripture quotations are taken from the *Holy Bible*, New Living Translation, copyright © 1996, 2004, 2015 Tyndale House Foundation. Used by permission of Tyndale House Publishers, Inc., Carol Stream, Illinois 60188. All rights reserved.

ISBN 978-1-4707-3919-5 Charcoal leather-like cover
ISBN 978-1-4707-3918-8 Turquoise leather-like cover
ISBN 978-1-4707-4272-0 Cranberry leather-like cover
ISBN 978-1-4707-4273-7 Saddle leather-like cover

Printed in China.

10 9 8 7 6 5 4 3   24 23 22 21 20 19 18 17 16